J 598.764 Ber
Berne, Emma Carlson
Hummingbirds : faster than
a jet!

DISCARD

$8.25
ocn833374556
First edition.   04/02/2014

ANIMAL SUPERPOWERS

HUMMINGBIRDS
Faster than a Jet!

Emma Carlson Berne

D1378875

PowerKiDS press™

New York

Published in 2014 by The Rosen Publishing Group, Inc.
29 East 21st Street, New York, NY 10010

First Edition

Editor: Joanne Randolph
Book Design: Kate Vlachos

Photo Credits: Cover Adam Jones/Photo Researchers/Getty Images; p. 4 ktsdesign/Shutterstock.com; p. 5 Eugato/Shutterstock.com; p. 6 Brian Lasenby/Shutterstock.com; p. 7 (sidebar) Glenn Price/Shutterstock.com; p .7 Mark Caunt/Shutterstock.com; p. 8 © iStockphoto.com/Giovanni Banfi; p. 9 © iStockphoto.com/estelle75; pp. 10, 18 Birdiegal/Shutterstock.com; p. 11 by Stephen Laczynski; pp. 12–13 iStockphoto/Thinkstock; p. 14 Charles Brutlag/Shutterstock.com; p. 15 yuqun/Shutterstock.com; p. 16 Sari ONeal/Shutterstock.com; p. 17 James Pierce/Shutterstock.com; pp. 19, 21 Michael Layefsky/Flickr/Getty Images; p. 20 Frank Pali/ Shutterstock.com; p. 21 (sidebar) Steve Byland/Shutterstock.com; p. 22 Christine Glade/E+/Getty Images. Interactive eBook Only: p. 4 lexaarts/Shutterstock.com; p. 8 © iStockphoto.com/David Ferry; p. 10 Jason David/iStockfootage/Getty Images; p. 11 DansPhotoArt on Flickr/Flickr/Getty Images; p. 14 Love Mushroom/ Shutterstock.com; p. 17 © Mercieca, Anthony/Animals, Animals; p. 19 Ed Reschke/Peter Arnold/Getty Images; p. 20 NightHorse Media Inc./Image Bank Film/Getty Images.

Library of Congress Cataloging-in-Publication Data

Berne, Emma Carlson.
 Hummingbirds: faster than a jet! / by Emma Carlson Berne. — First edition.
    pages cm. — (Animal superpowers)
 Includes index.
 ISBN 978-1-4777-0750-0 (library binding) — ISBN 978-1-4777-0841-5 (pbk.) —
 ISBN 978-1-4777-0842-2 (6-pack)
 1. Hummingbirds—Juvenile literature. I. Title.
 QL696.A558B475 2014
 598.7'64—dc23
                          2012047145

Manufactured in the United States of America

CPSIA Compliance Information: Batch #S13PK6: For Further Information contact Rosen Publishing, New York, New York at 1-800-237-9932

Contents

A Magical Bird 4

So Many Hummingbirds 6

Hummingbird Homes 8

Dining on Nectar 10

Facts About Hummingbirds 12

Amazing Wings 14

Hummingbird for Dinner, Anyone? 16

Getting Ready for Babies 18

Baby Hummingbirds.. 20

Long, Risky Flights...22

Glossary...23

Index 24

Websites 24

A Magical Bird

Imagine a tiny bird, colored bright green, ruby red, violet, and brilliant blue. This bird drinks from flowers, does acrobatics in midair, and appears and disappears as though by magic. Does this sound like an animal from a fairy tale? It is not. It is a hummingbird.

Hummingbirds can hover in the air as they drink nectar from flowers. Sometimes small hummingbirds are mistaken for bees because their wings move so fast they are hard to see.

Hummingbirds are tiny, delicate, and beautiful. They also have amazing superpowers. They are strong and fast. Hummingbirds can fly 500 miles (805 km) without stopping. They can live so high in the mountains that humans would get sick from the lack of **oxygen**. Some hummingbirds will visit 1,000 flowers a day to look for food. Let's visit the world of the hummingbird together.

Hummingbirds are known for their beautiful feathers.

So Many Hummingbirds

There are about 341 **species** of hummingbirds. All have long, slim beaks that they use to drink **nectar** from flowers. They have short legs and amazing wings that beat in a fast, figure-eight pattern. These **flexible** wings let the hummingbird hover in midair and fly backward.

Ruby-throated hummingbirds are the only hummingbirds that breed in eastern North America. They can be up to 3.5 inches (9 cm) long with a wingspan of around 4 inches (10 cm).

FASTEST ANIMAL ON EARTH

The fastest hummingbird is the Anna's hummingbird. This little bird moves at about 385 times its own body length per second. This is compared to a falcon's speed of 200 body lengths per second. A fighter jet with its afterburners on moves at only 150 body lengths per second!

All hummingbirds are small. The bee hummingbird is only about 2 ¼ inches (5.7 cm) long! Most hummingbirds have at least some beautiful, bright feathers. The male Calliope hummingbird has a green head and brilliant red feathers extending down from his beak onto his chest. The broad-billed hummingbird shimmers blue and green all over and has a pink beak.

Sword-billed hummingbirds live in South America. They live in Bolivia, Colombia, Ecuador, Peru, and Venezuela. They are named for their superlong bills. They are the only hummingbirds with bills longer than their bodies.

Hummingbird Homes

Where Hummingbirds Live

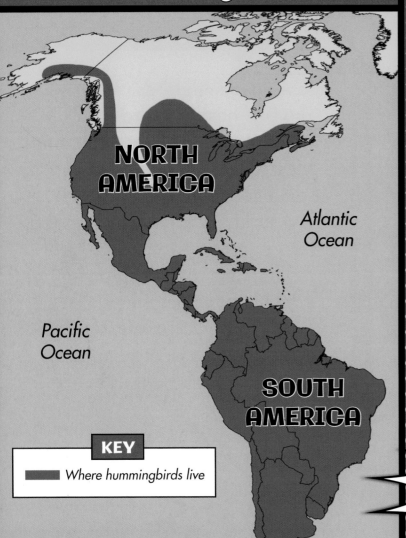

NORTH AMERICA

SOUTH AMERICA

Atlantic Ocean

Pacific Ocean

KEY
Where hummingbirds live

Hummingbirds live only in the **Western Hemisphere**. They can be found from Alaska all the way to Chile, at the tip of South America. They can live high in the mountains or in the steamy tropics. Hummingbirds often visit backyard feeders and gardens.

This map shows where in the world hummingbirds live. As you can see, they live only in North America, Central America, and South America.

This hummingbird lives in the West Indies, which are islands south of Florida.

Hummingbirds do not live in grasslands, in the desert, or in very thick forests. These places don't have enough flowers for them to find the food they need. Hummingbirds **migrate**, or move around to different places, depending on when flowers are blooming.

Dining on Nectar

Hummingbirds' long, thin beaks are perfect for reaching deep inside trumpet-shaped flowers to drink their nectar.

A hummingbird hovers close to a blossom and dips its long beak into the flower. It is drinking nectar, the sugary liquid made by plants. Hummingbirds use their forked tongues to lap up this sweet food. They need to eat a lot to stay alive. In one day, a hummingbird might eat up to three times its own body weight in nectar.

For protein, hummingbirds eat small insects and spiders. They also drink tree sap, which is sugary, like nectar. Hummingbirds can't bore holes in trees to get at the sap. Instead they use holes made by woodpeckers.

Many people have hummingbird feeders in their yards so they can see hummingbirds feeding up close. Hummingbird feeders are filled with a sugar mixture similar to nectar found in flowers.

FACTS ABOUT HUMMINGBIRDS

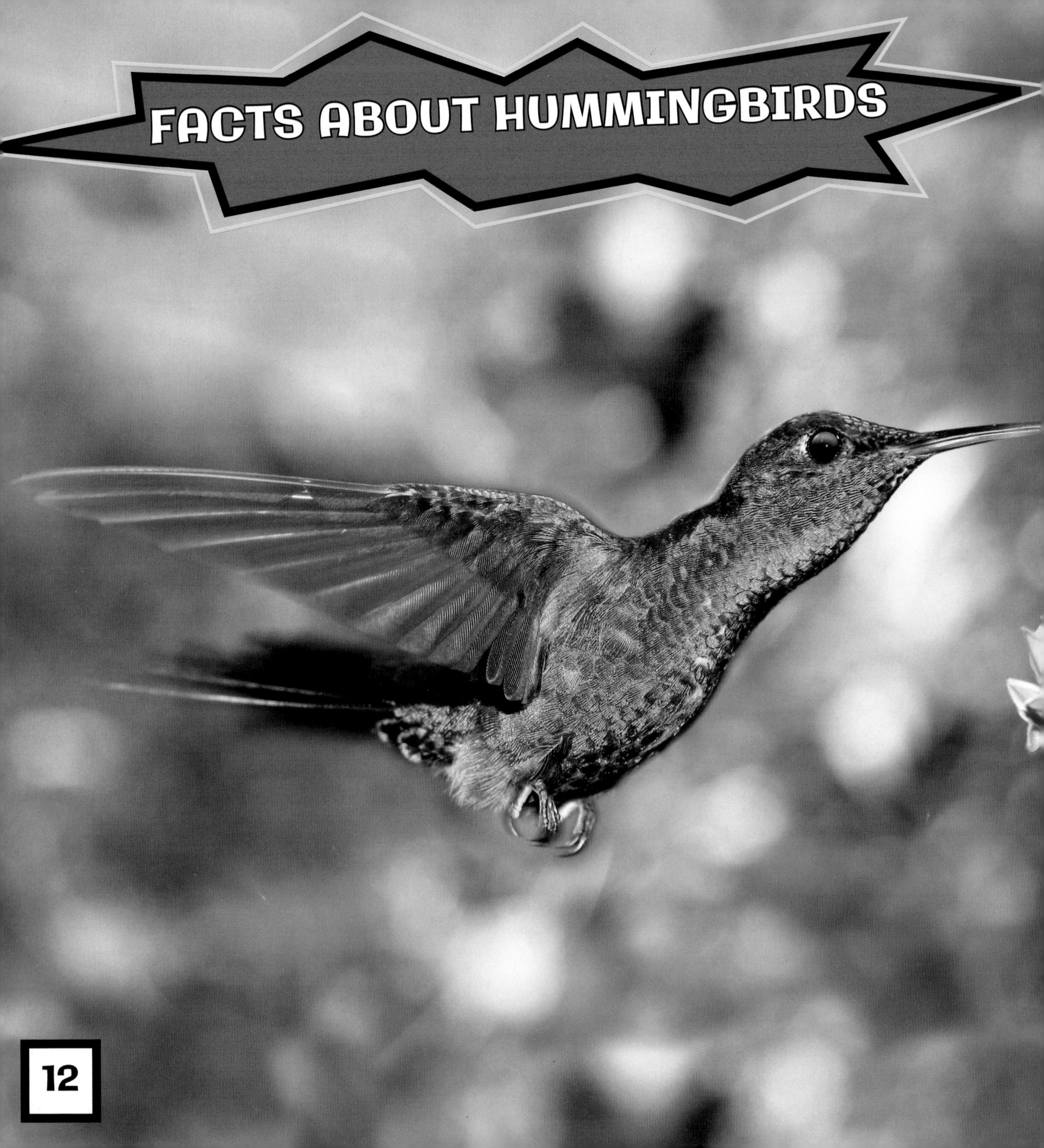

1 Hummingbirds can not only hover in midair and fly forward and backward, they can even briefly fly upside-down.

2 The Calliope hummingbird migrates about 2,800 miles (4,506 km) each year. When you compare how small the Calliope is with the length of the journey, that's the longest migration of any bird on Earth.

3 Hummingbirds lay the smallest eggs of any bird on the planet. Some are as small as a pea or a jellybean.

4 In the 1800s, women used to wear dead, stuffed hummingbirds on their hats. This was a very popular fashion.

5 When a hummingbird is resting, its heart beats about 500 times per minute. When it is excited, its heart rate zooms up to 1,200 beats per minute. The average heart rate for a person is about 75 beats per minute. The maximum for a person is between 160 and 220 beats per minute.

6 To eat as much as a hummingbird, you would have to eat 3,500 pancakes or a 5-pound (2 kg) bag of sugar every 40 minutes, every day.

Amazing Wings

Hummingbird wings beat so fast, they look like a blur. Bigger hummingbirds might beat their wings about 10 beats per second. Smaller ones might beat theirs 80 times a second. When a ruby-throated hummingbird is trying to attract a **mate**, his wing-beat rate can reach 200 beats per second!

Hummingbirds get their name because of the sound their superfast wings make as they are beating.

The reason hummingbirds can fly so fast is that they use their wings differently from other birds. Most birds have flexible wings and move their joints when they fly. Hummingbirds, though, hold their short wings stiffly. They move them the same way you move oars while rowing a boat. This movement gives them more power for flying.

It takes a special camera to get a picture in which we can see a hummingbird's wings clearly.

Hummingbird for Dinner, Anyone?

Pet cats are one of the main predators of hummingbirds.

Since hummingbirds are so small, they are a favorite snack for **predators**. Only some animals are fast enough to catch these little birds, though. Hawks can sometimes catch and eat hummingbirds.

Blue jays will sometimes make a meal out of small birds, such as hummingbirds.

On the ground, frogs, snakes, lizards, and cats sneak up on hummingbirds and snare them. Some large fish, like **bass**, can snatch a hummingbird if the bird flies too close to the surface of the water. Even some insects, like praying mantises and large ants, will catch and eat a small hummingbird if they can.

Getting Ready for Babies

Hummingbirds spend most of their lives alone. When it is time to have babies, though, the female hummingbird looks for a mate. Males will try to get her attention by showing off their feathers or doing fancy flying tricks and dives.

The hummingbird mother builds the nest and then sits on her eggs until they hatch. This can take from two to three weeks. The mother will leave the nest for short periods to eat.

The female hummingbird builds a nest by herself. Hummingbird nests are like stretchy little cups. The hummingbird uses bark, moss, leaves, or grass for the outside. She ties it all together with spiderwebs. Then she lines the inside of the nest with feathers or soft fur. After that, it's time to lay eggs!

Hummingbirds lay between one and three eggs in the nest. This is the nest of an Anna's hummingbird.

Baby Hummingbirds

The hummingbird eggs are ready to hatch in two to three weeks. The babies tap their way through the shells with the special tips on their beaks, called **egg teeth**.

The babies' little eyes are sealed shut when they are born. The babies don't have any feathers either, so their mother keeps them warm with her own body.

Mother hummingbirds feed their babies for a few weeks before the babies are big enough to find their own food.

G-FORCE

Hummingbirds make spectacular dives when they are flying. When they pull up from these dives, they experience 10 g, which is 10 times the force of gravity. By comparison, race car drivers, whose cars go from 0 to 100 miles per hour (0–161 km/h) in under a second, experience only 5 g.

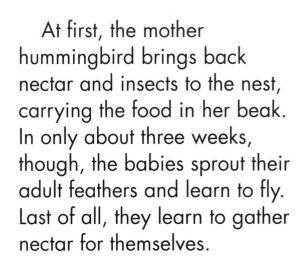

At first, the mother hummingbird brings back nectar and insects to the nest, carrying the food in her beak. In only about three weeks, though, the babies sprout their adult feathers and learn to fly. Last of all, they learn to gather nectar for themselves.

This Anna's hummingbird has just hatched from its egg.

Long, Risky Flights

Twice a year, most North American hummingbirds migrate from the south to the north and back again. These flights are very far. Many hummingbirds cross the **Gulf of Mexico** during their migration. To do this, they fly 500 miles (805 km) without stopping, which takes them about 20 hours. Hummingbirds can starve or freeze to death during their migration.

Hummingbirds are at risk in other ways, too. When wild areas are **cultivated**, hummingbirds can lose their **habitat**. Nearly 10 percent of all hummingbird species are threatened with **extinction**.

Most ruby-throated hummingbirds spend the winter somewhere between southern Mexico and Panama.

Glossary

bass (BAS) A type of fish that lives in both fresh and salt water and preys on other fish and small animals.

cultivated (KUL-tih-vayt-ed) To prepare land to grow crops for food.

egg teeth (EG TEETH) Sharp, toothlike parts on baby animals' beaks, used to crack open the eggshells.

extinction (ek-STINK-shun) The state of no longer existing.

flexible (FLEK-sih-bul) Moving and bending in many ways.

Gulf of Mexico (GULF UV MEK-sih-koh) A part of the Atlantic Ocean that is surrounded by the United States, Mexico, and Cuba.

habitat (HA-buh-tat) The kind of land where an animal or a plant naturally lives.

mate (MAYT) A partner for making babies.

migrate (MY-grayt) To move from one place to another.

nectar (NEK-tur) A sweet liquid found in flowers.

oxygen (OK-sih-jen) A gas that has no color or taste and is necessary for people and animals to breathe.

predators (PREH-duh-terz) Animals that kill other animals for food.

species (SPEE-sheez) One kind of living thing. All people are one species.

Western Hemisphere (WES-tern HEH-muh-sfeer) The western half of Earth.

Index

A
Anna's hummingbird, 7

B
babies, 18, 20–21
backyard(s), 8
beak(s), 6–7, 10, 20–21
broad-billed hummingbird, 7

E
egg, 13, 19–20
extinction, 22

F
fairy tale, 4
feathers, 7, 18–21

flower(s), 4–6, 9–10
food, 5, 9, 10, 21

G
grasslands, 9

H
habitat, 22

I
insect, 11, 17, 21

M
males, 18
migration, 13, 22
mountains, 5, 8

N
nectar, 6, 10–11, 21

O
oxygen, 5

P
protein, 11

S
South America, 8
species, 6, 22

W
Western Hemisphere, 8
wings, 6, 14–15
woodpeckers, 11

Websites

Due to the changing nature of Internet links, PowerKids Press has developed an online list of websites related to the subject of this book. This site is updated regularly. Please use this link to access the list:
www.powerkidslinks.com/asp/hbird/